More Memories of Old

CHESSINGTON

Since my earlier book *Chessington Remembered* was published in 1999, readers have told me many new fascinating tales of Chessington's past. So it seemed a good idea to put some of them into a little keepsake companion book to go with my earlier volume, which, incredibly, is still selling more than 20 years since it was first published. Here is a small collection of stories and pictures from old Chessington which I hope will be enjoyed and cherished for years to come.
Mark Davison

Former pupils of Moor Lane School at a reunion held in the Saker Pavilion, Leatherhead Road, Chessington, in 2002

Acknowledgments

Lionel Joseph; Celia Morrison archives; members of the former Moor Lane School reunion group; archives of Graham Wood; archives of BR and M Morrison, of Auckland, New Zealand; the late David Tippett-Wilson; Tony Harcombe and family; John Mead of Mirrorpix, Watford; John Wells (brother of Julie Andrews); Sean Hawkins; David East and family. Nigel Davison, Roy Hobbs and Ray Lloyd (who died in 2020).

Bibliography

'Home – A Memoir of My Early Years' by Julie Andrews (W&N 2008); London Omninbus Traction Society (Les Stitson archives); Chessington Remembered; Hook Remembered; Hook Remembered Again; Surrey Comet; Leatherhead Advertiser; Mecklenburg-strelitz.org; Daniel Corston.

Cover photographs Front: Copt Gilders c1952 with a 265 bus. Back: A 65 bus at Chessington Zoo, September 1978.

Published by Mark Davison, North Bank, Smoke Lane, Reigate, Surrey RH2 7HJ. Tel 01737 221215.
email: mark.davison1@virgin.net
Printed by New Ink, Caterham.
First edition November 2020.
ISBN 978-0-9569987-4-3

Julie Andrews writes fondly in her book of her stays in Roebuck Road, Chessington

Bridge Road, Chessington, in the 1950s, looking west, near the Blackamoor's public house. The road was named after the prominent Surbiton Borough Council member, Alderman C.H. Bridge, mayor in 1941 and 1942, and not the railway bridge constructed just before the first trains ran to Chessington South and Chessington North in 1938. Alderman Bridge promoted the building of 250 much-needed new council homes between Clayton Road and Mansfield Road, Hook

Hook Road looking south towards Chessington in 1962. The Bridge Road roundabout had not then been constructed

Exiled Russian prince and princess

CHESSINGTON became the unlikely home of an exiled Russian prince and princess in the 1920s.

Prince Vladimir Galitzine and his Princess wife, Catherine, spent 14 years living in Garrison Lane. Their spacious home was often frequented by the exiled Russian community living in England.

The couple and their three sons lived at Chessington Hall, near St Mary's Church. Their home in later years became the headquarters of Chessington British Legion before it was pulled down and replaced. So how did two members of the Russian Imperial royal family come to be in Chessington?

The princess was born in 1891 in Oranienbaum, her family's palatial estate near today's St Petersburg on the Gulf of Finland. Raised as the Countess Catherine of Carlow, (the Russian form of her name being Ekaterina Georgievna) she was the eldest child of Duke Georg Alexander and his wife, Countess Natalia Fedorovna, of Carlow. She was christened into the Lutheran church.

It is said she enjoyed an idyllic childhood in late Imperial Russia at her family's vast palace and at the family's St Petersburg river embankment mansion, 46 Fontanka.

As the grand-daughter of Grand Duchess Ekaterina Mikhailovna of Russia, she belonged to the most junior branch of the Russian Imperial family, descending from her great-grandfather, Grand Duke Mikhail Pavlovich of Russia, the youngest son of Emperor Pavel. As such, Countess Catherine was closely related to the ruling Romanov dynasty and a member of the imperial court. She was passionate about music and hosted many concerts at her home by notable musicians. Her father died in 1909 and she was brought up by her uncle, Duke Carl Michael.

In February 1913, in St Petersburg, Countess Catherine married Prince Vladimir Emanuelovich Galitzine. She adopted her husband's Russian Orthodox faith. In December that year, the couple welcomed

Princess Catherine Galitzine who lived for 14 years at Garrison Lane, Chessington

Prince Vladimir Galitzine

their first son, Prince Nikolai. During the First World War, Prince Galitzine was a captain in the Imperial Russian Army and served as aide-de-camp to Grand Duke Nikolai Nikolaevich of Russia, the commander-in-chief of the Russian Armies. Princess Catherine's war efforts included producing bandages and bed-clothes in sewing workshops and working in Red Cross depots.

She also opened a recuperation hospital at her home for recovering officers injured in the war. In May 1915 she joined her husband in Tiflis (now Tbilisi) in the Georgian Governate of the Russian Empire. It was here in April 1916 the couple welcomed their second son, Prince Georgii.

In 1917, with the abdication of Emperor Nikolai II and the abolition of the monarchy, the situation in Russia rapidly deteriorated as the country descended into a civil war fought between the Boleshviks and the anti-communist White Army.

Princess Catherine and her family sought refuge in Kislovodsk in the White Army-occupied Caucasus region of Russia. There, they were joined by other family members. It was here in May 1918 that her youngest son, Prince Emanuel, was born.

With the Bolsheviks' success in the Russian Civil War, it swiftly became evident that Princess Catherine and her young family had no future in Russia.

So faced with the advancing Red Army, they left their home country in April 1919 aboard the British ship HMS Grafton.

They changed ships in Constantinople and the family disemabarked in Italy and proceeded to make their way through France, where her mother, sister and brother initially settled, to the United Kingdom where Princess Catherine and her husband had decided to make their home.

It is thought that connections with Sir Francis Barker, of Chessington, who conducted business in Russia, were the instigator of the family moving to Chessington Hall. This rambling house, which had twice been rebuilt over the previous two centuries, was once the home of playwright Samuel Crisp and the authoress Fanny Burney was a frequent visitor to see Crisp.

Princess Catherine's sister and her children later joined them in Britian. It was in 1921 that Princess Catherine and Prince Vladimir rented Chessington Hall and this became their home for the next 14 years.

It was a regular gathering place for exiled Russians in Britain. To support his family, Prince Vladimir initially tried his hand at chicken and turkey farming before opening a Russian art shop in Berkeley Square, London.

In February 1933, having been in the country for more than a decade, Prince Vladimir applied to the Home Secretary for naturalisation as a British citizen. Two months later, in April 1933, Prince Vladimir, along with his three sons, received their certificates of naturalisation and made their oaths of allegiance.

In 1935, the family left Chessington, moving into a house at 131 Croxted Road in West Dulwich, London.

In London, Princess Catherine and her her husband were prominent members of the Russian community and regulars on the London social scene.

Princess Catherine was also actively engaged in charitable causes in support of the Russian Orthodox Church and the Russian Red Cross Society which provided support to Russian refugees living in Britian.

During the Second World War, Princess Catherine was again involved in the war effort. This time she worked as a civil servant in the Postal Censorship Department in London.

Tragically, on 8th October, 1940, she was seriously injured while on her way to work when the bus she was travelling in down Grays Inn Road was hit by a bomb in a German raid. She died later that day at the Royal Free Hospital. She was 49.

Her funeral was held on 10th October at the Russian Orthodox Church on Buckingham Palace Road, London, in the presence of her widower, three sons, sister and brother–in–law.

Among the notable attendees were members of the exiled Russian imperial family and nobility.

Following the funeral, Princess Catherine was buried in Brompton Cemetery. She left an estate to her husband worth just over £400 pounds. That's about £20,000 by today's values.

Barkers' links with Russia

Mark Barker

THE Barker family, of Barwell Court and formerly of Chessington Hall, were prominent figures in Chessington. Alfred Barker, who died in 1922 aged 57, was a banker in Constantinople, where his son, Francis, was born. Francis became one of the foremost international traders of the time, building up strong trading links with Russia. Mark, a son of Francis, was heavily involved in Chessington life and became a councillor. He died in 2004 aged 73.

Vinod and Bee in 2009

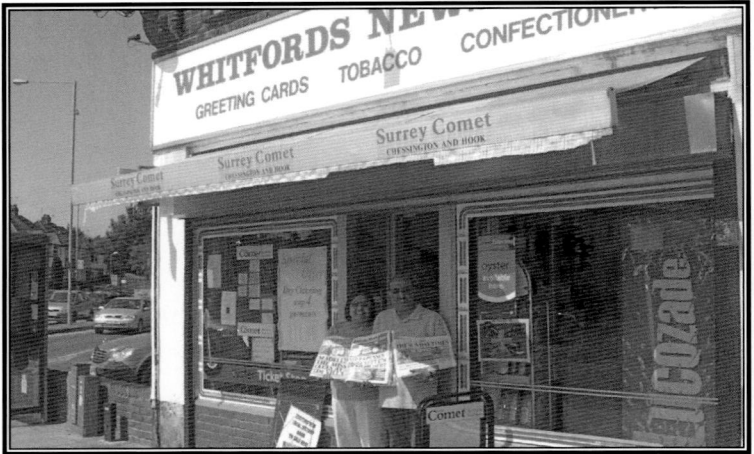

Newsagents for eight years

NEWSAGENTS Vinod and Bee Parmar served many hundreds of customers during their eight years at Whitford's Newsagents in North Parade, Chessington.

They came to the shop in July 2001 and worked tirelessly until their departure date for pastures new. Their final day at Whitford's was 5th June 2009.

Vinod previously worked at Heathrow Airport in baggage handling and his wife in a pharmaceutical office in Middlesex, close to their home in Waverley Road, Harrow. Vinod was first introduced to his wife through a relative. Vinod came to the UK from Kenya when he was aged 11 in 1972. He was born in Uganda. His schooling was in Leicester.

On their final day, Bee told customers: "We have made lots of friends in Chessington and learnt a lot about the retail business."

Vinod said: "We've met all sorts of people from all walks of life."

In 2009 the couple had three children: Bijal, 23, a school teacher in Stanmore, Middlesex; Heena, 20, who was studying forensic science and criminolgy at Middlesex University; and Hanish, 19, who was studying IT. In 2020, Vinod was working at Heathrow again; Bee part-time at an Iceland store in Harrow. "I miss Chessington," she said.

Lionel Joseph's mother Agnes (holding child) with friends and family at the junction of Chessington Road and Ruxley Lane in 1917

My boyhood memories of Hook

LIFE in Chessington and Hook almost a century ago was far different from now. Imagine a school caretaker today cooking potato skins on top of the school boiler for his chickens. Or being the victim of a catapult ink-bombing in the classroom. Or even going to the grocer's and asking for a box of broken biscuits.

In 2020, at the age of 97, retired school teacher Lionel Joseph reminisced about his schooldays in Hook back in the early 1930s. He was born on 12th August, 1923 and had crystal-clear memories of his boyhood. The family of seven lived in a cottage called Bon Aventure, off Chessington Road, West Ewell – near Scott's Farm in Ruxley Lane. Joseph used to walk each day to Hook School, Orchard Road – now more commonly known as St Paul's School.

"One pupil I remember well was Betty Yates. Her family lived on the Chessington Road – on the south side just past the Bonesgate pub. She had a sister, Joan, and a younger brother. Joan was called up for the Land Army and was working, as were many other Land Army girls, locally. She married a reserve occupation farm worker, as did many of those young girls. Betty Reynolds, as she became, and her husband became the owners of Ives Farm, close to Ruxley Lane, in the early 1950s and a couple of years later sold the farm to the Knight family.

"At Hook School, there was an enormous Douglas fir tree in the school forecourt. One year the school boiler broke down and we had three days of extra 'holiday'. Sometimes, the caretaker cooked potato peelings on top of the boiler and took them to his chicks at afternoon playtime.

The school staged its annual prize-giving ceremonies those days in the old vicarage in Hook Road, almost opposite Hook Parish Church. The headmaster at the time was Arthur Harrold. The vicar was the Reverend William Featherstone, who served the parish between 1932 and 1944. The old Victorian vicarage was pulled down in 1959 and a new home for the vicars and their families was built next to the church opposite.

"In my last year at Hook School, I was the recipient of one such prize. It was a lovely afternoon and we were all arrayed in a half circle, sitting on the grass with a pile of books on a table in front of me. In that pile was one about trains which attracted my attention. When called forward, it was presented to me. Goodness knows why. As far as I know, I had done nothing to deserve it, especially as often when the vicar was taking my class for religious knowledge – amounting to learning the Lord's Prayer and the Creed by heart – I was often spending the time in the 'naughty corner' behind the piano.

Lionel Joseph, far right, in 1926 with his siblings, left to right, Lorna, Marian, Leslie and Winifred. INSET: Lionel at 97

The Joseph family had a Humber motor car in the late 1920s and would often be seen pootling around the roads of Chessington and Hook

"I would dip my pen in the ink-well and flick the ink up into the rafters. One splash of ink was stuck high up there for years. Paper pellets were dipped in the ink-wells before delivery. Using a strong elastic band as a catapult, I hit one girl who was doing her needle-work and received severe punishment as a result."

Mr Joseph was fascinated to read in *Hook Remembered Again* a story about the Holford family, who lived at Southernhay, 207 Hook Road – where famous children's author Enid Blyton had taught and written her first children's book of verse in the early 1920s.

The Holfords owned a Morgan car in the 1930s which was very noisy.

"A cousin of mine, Ben Croft, was living in Camberwell, and upon marriage bought a house in the new [Rhodrons Avenue] estate off Elm Road, Hook. He was a civil engineer responsible for Fulham Power Station, and later the Asswan High Dam on the Nile in Egypt at the time of the Suez crisis. He became somewhat imprisoned, and was taken everywhere by an army motorcyclist with a sidecar. The work at the dam was at a critical stage where the system to prevent silt accumulating behind the dam was taking place."

One morning at Hook, he was offered a lift in a Morgan car. They were travelling so fast along the Kingston bypass at Hook Rise North, Tolworth, that a terrible accident nearly occurred. It was too late to go around the roundabout and they went straight over it, carrying on to London.

The Holfords' Morgan in the year 2020 was still being driven by its owner in the north of England. Mr Joseph's twin sons went on to own their own Morgan vintage cars.

"Our twins own three Morgans between them. One, the 1926 aero model has the Anzio engine as used by Louis Blelot for the first cross-Channel flight."

Mr Jospeh fondly recalled Oakey's the grocer's in Hook Road, north of the Ace of Spades roundabout: "Oakey's did a morning round, col-lecting the orders, followed by an afternoon round delivering those orders. They sold large biscuit tins of broken biscuits direct from the manufacturers. They were cheap and much appreciated."

The Bonesgate pub in about 1920. Mr Joseph said that at that time there was a minor ford over the Bonesgate stream, a tributary of the Hogsmill river. The road bridge came in 1926 along with tarmac on the former sandy surface. The tar was sprayed still hot, from a tank and the surface chippings rolled in by a steam roller – a real steam one

Mr Joseph's wife of many years – Joyce – a Surbiton midwife in the 1940s whose story is recalled in the book *Fireside Tales of Tolworth* had her own tale to tell about the novelist Thomas Hardy, whose first marital home in 1874 was St David's Villa, 13 Hook Road.

"Joyce's grandparents lived in West Stafford, Dorset, close to Hardy's home when he lived in the south-west. Often when walking into

Hook roundabout at the 'Ace of Spades' in the 1930s

Dorchester, they met him and chatted."

Mr Joseph also enthused about the fact the internationally known singer, Petula Clark, was brought up in Salmons Road, Chessington, and noted: "Petula Clark had a sister, Peggy, who worked at the Pearl Assurance in Holborn and was a friend of Joyce when working, prior to her [Joyce] starting nursing at the age of 18."

Lionel Joseph remembered the early days of Hook Parish Hall which opened in 1926 next to the King Edward Recreation Ground, Hook Road.

"The hall was used by Hook School [St Paul's] for school productions. At the age of five, my eldest sister, Marian, was the Alice of A.A. Milne's Christopher Robin verse. And I was dressed up as Christopher Robin about which I was not too pleased. Another aspect was the putting on of an Eisteddfod in 1933. The master of ceremonies was Freddy Grisewood, who, at the time, was a BBC newsreader and announcer.

"One item in the programme was "A humorous song" and my father

The Joseph family's home in Ruxley Lane, West Ewell, from where Lionel walked daily to Hook School via Moor Lane

set me up for that. As the only entrant, I was awarded the bronze medal duly inscribed on the obverse side. The song came out later under the title 'The Laughing Policeman' as a 78rpm wax record.

"My medal has been a source of amusement to my family ever since.

"The hall had a beautiful floor of either strip or narrow boards on which a large quantity of French chalk was scattered for an evening dance on a Friday or Saturday evening. We kids were apt to use it as a slide of some length.

"There were also flower shows. In my final year at Hook School, we had allotment plots for gardening lessons and were encouraged to enter the shows. But if it stipulated six potatoes, and on arrival home, two miles away, one potato was found in the bag, such entries did

Lionel Joseph's sister, Winifred, by the family's Renault 8hp tourer motor car. It was purchased from Welham's Garage at the foot of Surbiton Hill, which was the main Renault dealer at the time. The picture was taken in the Lake District in 1933. Lionel mused: "It was the sort of car that had a reverse gear lower than the first gear, and, so, on occasions would be turned around and reversed all the way up a steep hill. Such was a common sight on Sundays on Pebble Hill, near Box Hill."

not win prizes. It was at this time I was taught the overhand grasp of spades and shovels, so the strain is on the shoulder muscles, not the back. Hence, at 96 years of age, I can still 'turn the sods' as we were apt to say at Hook School. The Yetties' record 'Yetties of Westminster' has a poem, 'The Marrow'. It epitomises the Hook Flower Show. Happy days, long remembered!"

Mr Joseph's father, Harry, cycled daily to Worcester Park to get a train to his job at Mount Pleasant Royal Mail sorting office.

Marian Joseph with her husband Ted Rands and their toddler daughter during the 1940s in their Samdum sidecar which attached to bicycles to provide transport for a passenger. The sidecar was advertised for sale in Shipley Bridge, Horley, when Ted was away from home, serving in the Royal Navy. Marian's brother, Lionel, a keen cyclist, was asked to pick it up. He pedalled more than 25 miles to Shipley Bridge, and then, with sidecar attached, he cycled home to Ewell. "I rode the whole lot up Reigate Hill and then it was mainly down-hill. I had to take the sidecar off the bike that night because I was off at 6am to cycle to work in London. That was a 36-mile round trip." In the year 2020, at the age of 97, Lionel still cycled regularly around his home at Forest Green, Dorking.

Chessington Youth Club 1947

Chessington Youth Club was formed just after the Second World War at Moor Lane School. This picture was taken in the school hall in 1947/8

Fun and games at Moor Lane School in the mid-1940s

Pupils at Moor Lane School took to the stage in the early 1950s. In 1952 they performed Bernard Shaw's Androcles and The Lion, and in 1953, Shaw's St Joan

The football team at Chessington Youth Club, Moor Lane School, in 1948. Members included J. Nouch, Dave King, Don Biggs, C. Fairman, K. Edwards, B. Morrison, J. Woodger, R. Richards and B. Campbell. Some of the players later moved 'down under'. Dave King and Bernard Morrison lived in New Zealand; R. Richards and B. Campbell settled in Australia. These photos came from the archives of Mr Morrison, who in 2000 was living in Onehunga, Auckland.

Staff at Lovelace School, Mansfield Road, Hook, in the early 1980s

Two photographs showing the soccer and cricket teams at Moor Lane School in 1948. In the bottom picture, the headmaster, Mr Loveless, top left, is seen with some of the members including teacher Mr Rollie, and pupils J. Brown, A. Haggis, M. Chilcott, D. Biggs, D.P. Biggs and and J. Gale.

The tanker MV Magdala was sunk without trace in January 1945

Moor Lane pupil, 16, dies at war

A FORMER Moor Lane School pupil was killed at the age of 16 in the Second World War. He was Royston Haggis, son of Sidney and Dorothy Haggis, of 1 Hartfield Road, Hook.

In mid January 1945, the Dutch steel tanker Magdala, built in 1931 by Van Der Giessen C. & Zonen and owned at the time of her loss by Petroleum Maatschappij La Corona N.V., left Rejkjavik for Belfast in ballast, and went missing.

The Magdala has not been heard of ever since. Thirty-five people lost their lives. She was in the storm-scattered convoy RU-150 and may have been torpedoed by U-boat 1051 or 1055.

Royston was a cabin boy on the Magdala, serving with the Merchant Navy when the boat sank on January 15, 1945.

He is commemorated on the Tower Hill Memorial in London.

Royston's brother, A. Haggis, played for the Moor Lane School cricket team. There was another son, Donald, born in July 1929.

A class of 1951 at Moor Lane School, Chessington

A Moor Lane School outing in 1951

Pupils at Moor Lane School performing Androcles and the Lion, based on George Bernard Shaw's play, in 1950

Early days of Moor Lane near the junction of Church Lane. The 65A bus formerly used Church Lane before switching to Gilders Road

Another class from 1951 at Moor Lane School, and below, a choir at the school rehearsing

People in Chessington and Hook have fond memories of shopping at Wendy's, 440 Hook Road near Mansfield Road. Here they would go for their wool and baby clothes

*The Stokes family of Sherborne Road were keen motorcyclists. Here,
Brian, Alan and Ken Stokes are seen with one of their gleaming
machines in about 1958*

A further class picture from 1951 at Moor Lane School

Freddie Phillips in 1948 on his special eight-stringed guitar

Freddie was, in earlier years, spelled Freddy

Music for Trumpton created at Chessington Road home

Pugh, Pugh, Barney, McGrew, Cuthbert, Dibble, Grubb...

THE memorable 1960s children's TV series Camberwick Green, Trumpton and Chigley had an unlikely link with Chessington. For the episodes featured the music of a classically-trained guitarist who lived a few hundred yards from the Bonesgate public house at the end of Moor Lane. And at least three episodes of Trumpton were recorded in his house.

The music to the scenes showing stop-go stringless puppets in the three series of programmes broadcast between January 1966 and October 1969 was provided by Freddie Phllips whose home was at 178 Chessington Road.

Freddie Phillips composed and played the music which was sung and narrated by the late Brian Cant. It is believed that all the songs were recorded at Phillips' home in Chessington Road.

Children in the Sixties will fondly recall Camberwick Green's characters including Windy Miller, Dr Mopp, Mickey Murphy, PC McGarry, Peter Hazel and the rest.

" The show brings to children the elements of life in a typical English village," the show's creator, Gordon Murray, who worked as a professional puppeteer for the BBC, wrote on the sleeve notes to the LP record "Welcome to Camberwick Green" which was contemporaneously released.

The Trumptonshire Trilogy website devoted to the 39 episodes of the three series, states: "For Trumps, he [Brian Cant] recorded three full episodes in a single day at Freddie Phillips' house in Chessington, which doubled as a makeshift studio – a suitably Heath Robinson affair, as befitted the cottage industry nature of the whole production with frequent pauses in recording caused by aircraft noise. Not that you'd know it from the iconic end results of course".

The first episode of Camberwick Green featured Peter the Postman. Gordon Murray's puppets in Camberwick Green left children spell-bound as they went about their business in a little sleepy market town. He wrote the scripts and made most of the characters, all of which were no more than six inches tall. The sets were created by

No 178 Chessington Road (far right) was the home of the "Trumpton" musician Freddie Phillips

Freddie Phillips at home in Chessington Road in 1970

husband and wife team, John and Margaret Brownfoot, whose background was in theatrical design. All the sets were stored in a single room of their home in Harrow Hill, north-west London. The animation was executed by Bob Bura and John Hardwick and their team. Both were ex-colleagues of Gordon Murray at the BBC.

Most of the filming was carried out at a disused church in Crouch Hill, London, later purchased by the Eurythmics pop duo.

According to The Trumpton Trilogy, all three series were originally shot in both colour and black and white. The BBC did not introduce colour until 1969.

Gordon Murray once explained why there was no fourth series. "Although I toyed with the idea of a fourth series, using a suitable seaside location, I felt the Trumptonshire programmes had run their natural course."

Every single song and sound effect was composed and/or performed by classically trained guitarist Phillips, the Trumptonshire Trilogy website states. "All were recorded in his home... in between frequent interruptions for under-the-flightpath aircraft noise!"

Following his death, Freddie Phillips' son, John, held all the rights to the music. And it is the only part of Trumptonshire that Gordon Murray's estate does not hold the copyright to, the website states. Brian Cant died aged 83 in June 2017. Gordon Murray died in June 2016, aged 95.

Frederick Phillips passed away in Ewell on October 4, 2003, aged 84. He was born on August 2, 1919. He and his wife, Audrey, married in Surrey in 1943. Mrs Phillips passed away in the year 2000. They were residents of Chessington Road for more than 50 years.

In 1999, Gypsy Jazz publication carried an article about Freddie Phillips.

In his piece, Peter Senster wrote that Phillips began his musical life at the age of 17 when he bought his first guitar. Teaching himself, he attempted to play all the music he could lay his hands on, including books of violin and clarinet studies. His early professional engagements, included the International Sporting Club, Monte Carlo; the Hotel Bristol, Oslo; and Lyons Corner House, London. He worked hard

Welcome to CAMBERWICK GREEN

A Visit to Trumpton

From the B.B.C. Television 'Watch With Mother' series

The Music for Pleasure albums featuring the music of Freddie Phillips in 1967

to perfect his sight-reading and began to develop his "plectrum-plus-fingers" technique, based on old Spanish methods for the "vihuela de pendola" (viola plucked with a quill – one of the forerunners of the modern guitar) which was played with both right-hand fingers and a quill (or plectrum). This style of playing increased his scope for correct interpretation of his transcriptions of the works of Bach, Mozart, Manuel de Fallaand the like. The Second World War years saw him serve with the Field Ambulance Infantry and, in 1943, with the British Band of the AEF under George Melachrino in which organisation he was frequently on the radio both as a soloist and a member of the Ronnie Selby (Piano) Trio. Freddie Phillips' efficiency at sight-reading and his ability to interpret all types of music brought him radio work with orchestras of many widely divergent styles as Harry Gold, Ted Heath, Monia Liter and Eugene Pini. Latterly he was heard frequently with his own quintet and his trio of two guitars and bass which mainly featured music of Latin origin.

"As an accompanist and as a dispenser of background music, he is much in evidence on both BBC radio and television programmes. Recently he broke new ground with his original television play, "The Eye of the Gypsy," providing the entire background music on solo guitar for which he received the plaudits of the critics."

Phillips also wrote and performed the music for all six episodes of Gordon Murray's short-lived stop-motion television eeries, "Rubovia". In its March 1995 issue, "Total Guitar" magazine published an interesting article showing the reader how to play the Trumpton Firemen Theme "Firemen Bold". Joe Bennett, the magazine's technical/music editor and author of the article, describes it as "an example of how you can find great guitar playing in the unlikeliest of places".

Phillips co-wrote some of the lyrics and created all of the sound effects for the Trumptonshire series – such as the memorable sound of Windy's mill turning. For many people it was the music and songs that made the Trumpton series so memorable.

"More than 30 years after it was written, the Trumptonshire music still generates considerable media interest (such as the BBC 'Smallpeople' promotional film), and even late in his life he still kept his hand in with the classical guitar. In 1999, he seemed well aware of how popular the Trumptonshire music had been, and how people still fondly remember it – Pugh, Pugh, Barney McGrew, Cuthbert, Dibble, Grubb.

It was Phillips who added the second 'Pugh' to the line-up in order to get the rhythm to work.

Phillips said in an interview: "Gordon Murray called his contributors his 'cottage industries' and that is what we were. All animation was done in a 'small backroom' as, I believe, were the set designs. An upstairs room in my house was divided by sound-proof partitions; two-thirds for the machines; one third for the recording cubicle. I supplied all the recording equipment including Wright and Weir, Brenell, Revox A77, Revox A700 master mixer, speakers, Senheiser mikes and reverb/echo boxes etcetera, especially for work on Trumptonshire."

The shopping parade at Copt Gilders soon after the Second World War. Many of the roads on the estate are named after villages in the Norfolk Broads. Most end with the letters "by": Stokesby, Hemsby, Rollesby, Billockby and the like. It is likely that the developers hailed from this part of Norfolk when the road names were suggested and then adopted.

Hollies visit the zoo

Top Manchester pop group The Hollies (above and bottom right) performed at Chessington Zoo early in their musical career. They were at the zoo promoting their new single "Here I Go Again". The visit took place on 26th May, 1964. The record reached number four in the hit parade. The band had already enjoyed chart success with the hits "Just Like Me", "Searching", "Stay", and "Just One Look".

Bygone days at Chessington Zoo

Jumbo the elephant seen taking the 65 bus at Chessington Zoo in August 1938

"Comet" the zoo's 20-year-old elephant, waking her keeper,
Philip Ashford, in July 1952

Ben, the zoo's hippo, who weighed a ton, having a plastic bag removed from its teeth on 17th July 1970

Hook Road, at the junction of Bridge Road, looking, towards Chessington Parade in 1962

Julie Andrews' time in Chessington

Julie Andrews spent some of her childhood in Roebuck Road

ACTRESS and singer Julie Andrews spent part of her childhood in Roebuck Road, Chessington. Her father, Ted Wells, lived at 15 Roebuck Road, in the 1940s and taught woodwork at Moor Lane School. Julie as a girl often used to stay at her father's house and would sometimes come to the school and be looked after by pupils while her father was teaching. Those days, her name was Julia Wells.

She was not a permanent resident of Roebuck Road as she chiefly lived with her mother, who was separated from her father.

Julie's brother, John, was a pupil at the school. Ted Wells married his new partner, Win, on 3rd June, 1944. Using a legacy that Win's father had left her, the couple bought the house at Roebuck Road. Win worked at the Esher Filling Station.

Julie Andrews later wrote: "On my early visits to Chessington, I was resentful of the new woman in my dad's life, but she tried very hard to make my time there special. She was also a marvellous cook. While Win stayed home to prepare her meals, Dad would take us on expeditions. Johnny, then aged six, would ride on the back of Dad's bike and I would ride on my own. We'd go to the zoo, or we would cycle a fair distnce to Surbiton Lagoon – a big open-air swimming pool that was always perishingly cold. I wasn't used to the outdoor life and I would often feel weak and sickly. Life with Dad and Win and Johnny could seem a bit too robust."

ABOVE: Julie Andrews with her dad, Ted Wells, sister Celia, Win and Johnny Wells. RIGHT: Julie Andrews and brother Johnny, on a sledge in the late 1930s, and an early publicity shot

Julie learnt to swim at Surbiton Lagoon in Berrylands having been instructed by her father. "He was endlessly patient but every time he let go of me, I'd go under the surface, gasping and taking in great gulps of chlorinated water. Johnny, of course, swam easily and well. At the end of each lesson, Dad would leave Johnny and me in the shallow end while he went off to enjoy his own moment in the pool. He would climb to the topmost diving board in the deep end. 'There goes Dad,' we would say, waving and feeling so proud as he executed marvellous swan dives, pikes and jack-knives.

"Dad would then come and fetch us and give us a rough, brisk, tow-eldown. And by now we were all goosebumps and blue – and then he'd buy us each a hot chocolate and doughnut at the Lagoon cafe.

"It was a somewhat painful experience, struggling to learn to swim, with the water being so cold, being chilled to the marrow. But by the end of the morning, it felt so good to have done it and to have the treat afterwards. In spite of the long ride home, it was always worth the effort – quality time with Dad. I was promised a five-pound note the day I learned to swim. In those days, a "fiver" was a large piece of white paper, thin like tssue, engraved with a fine, beautiful calligraphy and with a tiny thread of steel running through it.

"I remember the day my feet finally came up off the bottom of the pool and there I was, swimming alone! Dad was thrilled. I was thrilled. We went home to tell Win the good news and we had a celebration lunch. I was duly given my fiver — it felt like a lot of money — and a great fuss was made over me. From then on, swimming was great."

Julie wrote that bedtime at Chessington was another painful experience: "Dad would tuck me up into bed and read me a poem or story, in his precise, beautifully modulated voice. I would lie there, watching as he leaned towards the bedside light, studying his profile, loving him so much, knowing that my return home was imminent and that he was giving me every ounce of himself that he possbly could. I would feel so sad and try not to cry, knowing that my tears would cause him grief. I'd pretend to fall asleep while he was reading, so that I wouldn't have to return his goodnight kiss or hug,

*Seen at Surbiton Lagoon in the 1940s are Julie Andrews, far
left, with her siblings, Johnny Wells, Donald, Celia and Chris.
The lagoon was a very popular lido where hundreds would
gather to splash around, eat ice cream and meet
others on sunny summer days. But Julie's memories are those
of freezing cold water in which she learnt to swim. She was
given a five-pounds reward when she finally could swim.*

for a gentle hug would have done me in altogether."

In October 2020, John Wells spoke briefly to the author of this book, confirming his father taught at Moor Lane School and as well as woodwork, his dad would occasionally give instruction in metalwork. John has spent his retirement in Leicestershire.

Back in the early 1940s, sad at the thought of returning home to Beckenham one day, Julie stared at a glass cut-glass bowl on the sideboard at the house in Roebuck Road

She recalled being transfixed by the rainbow refractions off the glass. "I thought that if I stared at it for long enough, it may have stopped me from crying. And Dad would say 'Chick, we'll get together again as soon as we possibly can.' He didn't speak much on the phone for that was painful, too. But he kept every promise and on whatever date he said he was coming for me, he came."

That autumn, Julie commenced schooling at the Cone-Ripman School in London. She stayed with an aunt in London, returning to Beckenham at the weekends.

Julie had family links with Walton on Thames. Her great-grandparents had lived at Hersham, where Julie's maternal grandmother, Julia Ward, was born in 1887.

Julie's mother, Barbara Ward Morris, was born in July 1910. Barbara's father had deserted the army after being based at Caterham Barracks in Surrey. The family moved to Kent after Arthur was released from prison for desertion and later the family relocated to South Yorkshire.

Arthur used to write poetry. He was also a musical entertainer. He taught Julie Andrews' mother to play the piano and she became a polished performer and entertainer. Barbara in 1924, aged 14, passed the London College of Music's senior level exams. She and her father used to tour on the entertainment circuit. She broadcast on the radio at Sheffield and was teaching music by the age of 16.

Julie was born on 1st October, 1935 at Rodney House, Walton on Thames – a maternity hospital. Her brother, John, arrived two and a half years later.

Julie's grandad, Arthur, spent years in Brookwood Sanitorium, near

near Woking, and had been adjudged to be "insane". This period was not often refrred to in family talks.

Ted Wells, Julie's father, was the son of carpenter David Wells, a coachman for a Lady Tilson, of Guildford. David's wife, Fanny, had relatives who kept a shop at Hersham. During a bad period of unemployment he cycled all the way from Hersham to Wales to seek work. It took him 16 hours.

Ted Wells received a scholarship to go to Tiffin School in Kingston. He drifted around building sites looking for work but took evening classes in Kingston to improve his talents. He became a full-time teacher at the age of 24 in December 1932 and the same day — Boxing Day — married Julie's mother at St Peter's Church, Hersham.

Officially a practical handicrafts teacher, Ted Wells gave lessons in woodwork, metalwork, basic construction and engineering. But he also "subbed" for other teachers, instructing in English literature, maths and grammar. Being a specialist, his roles were only one day a week here and one day a week there, around Surrey villages. After a full-time role at Chessington, he taught at Beare Green School near Dorking, living in rural Catt Lane, Ockley.

At one time he owned a motorbike but for years he cycled 200 miles a week around Surrey, teaching hither and thither. At the end of the 1932 term, he took home just £11 which had to last until the end of the following month. A full-time position at Shere was secured after his temporary work.

In 1937, the Wells family lived at Kenrya, a house in Thames Ditton, near the river. At the end of the 1930s, Julie's mother was often away touring with entertainer Ted Andrews who she first met at a show in Bognor in which they both performed. He was a Canadian tenor. They eventually became romantically involved and the marriage to Ted Wells was in jeopardy. Barbara Wells married Ted Andrews on 25th November, 1943 and Julie's surname was changed to Andrews. Julia became Julie in the process. Her acting career saw world-wide fame in her major roles in Mary Poppins and the Sound of Music in the 1960s. She lived in the USA in later life and celebrated her 85th birthday in October 2020.

King and Queen's visit in 1939

The King and Queen are welcomed at RAF Hook Balloon Barrage Station, Mansfield Road, on 16th April 1939

LESS than six months before the start of the Second World War, King George VI, his queen – the future Queen Mother – and the Prime Minister, Neville Chamberlain, visited RAF Hook Ballon Barrage Station. Some 45 acres of the Lovelace estate on the Chessington side of what became Mansfield Road was used to build the station in 1938 – one of 10 developed across the London area. Steel cables were designed to hang from the balloons at up to 25,000 ft to deter low-flying enemy aircraft in the event of war. The royal visitors and the premier were accompanied by Joseph Kennedy, the American Ambassador to the UK and father of John F Kennedy.

One of 50 barrage balloons planned to be stationed at Hook

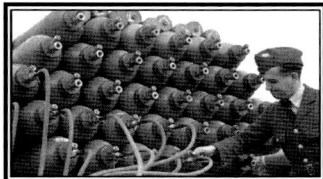

LEFT: Officers demonstrate how the balloons are inflated. ABOVE: Some of the gas canisters used

The royals are saluted as they arrive at the balloon station

The Prime Minister, Neville Chamberlain, wearing a grey bowler hat, chats with officials on the visit

The King greets officials from Hook Balloon Barrage Station

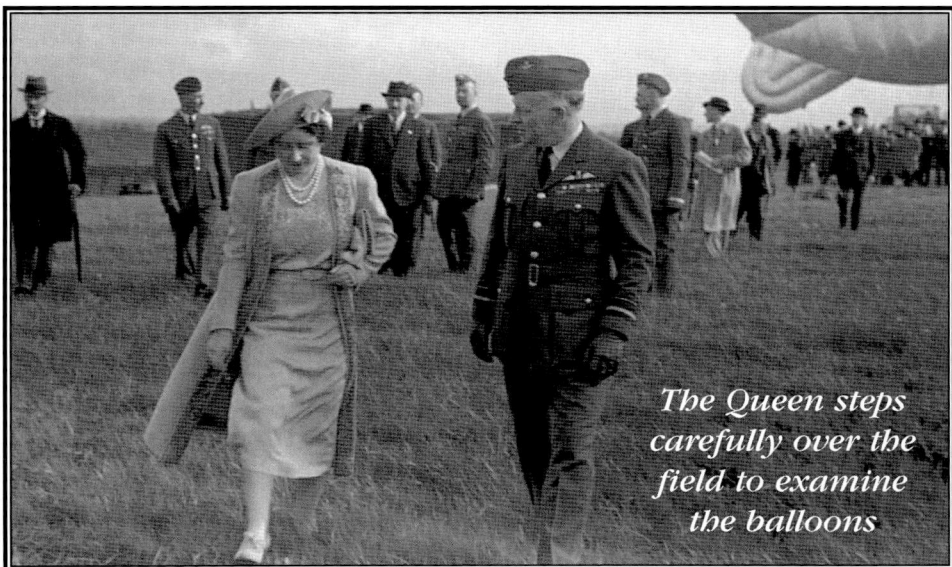

The Queen steps carefully over the field to examine the balloons

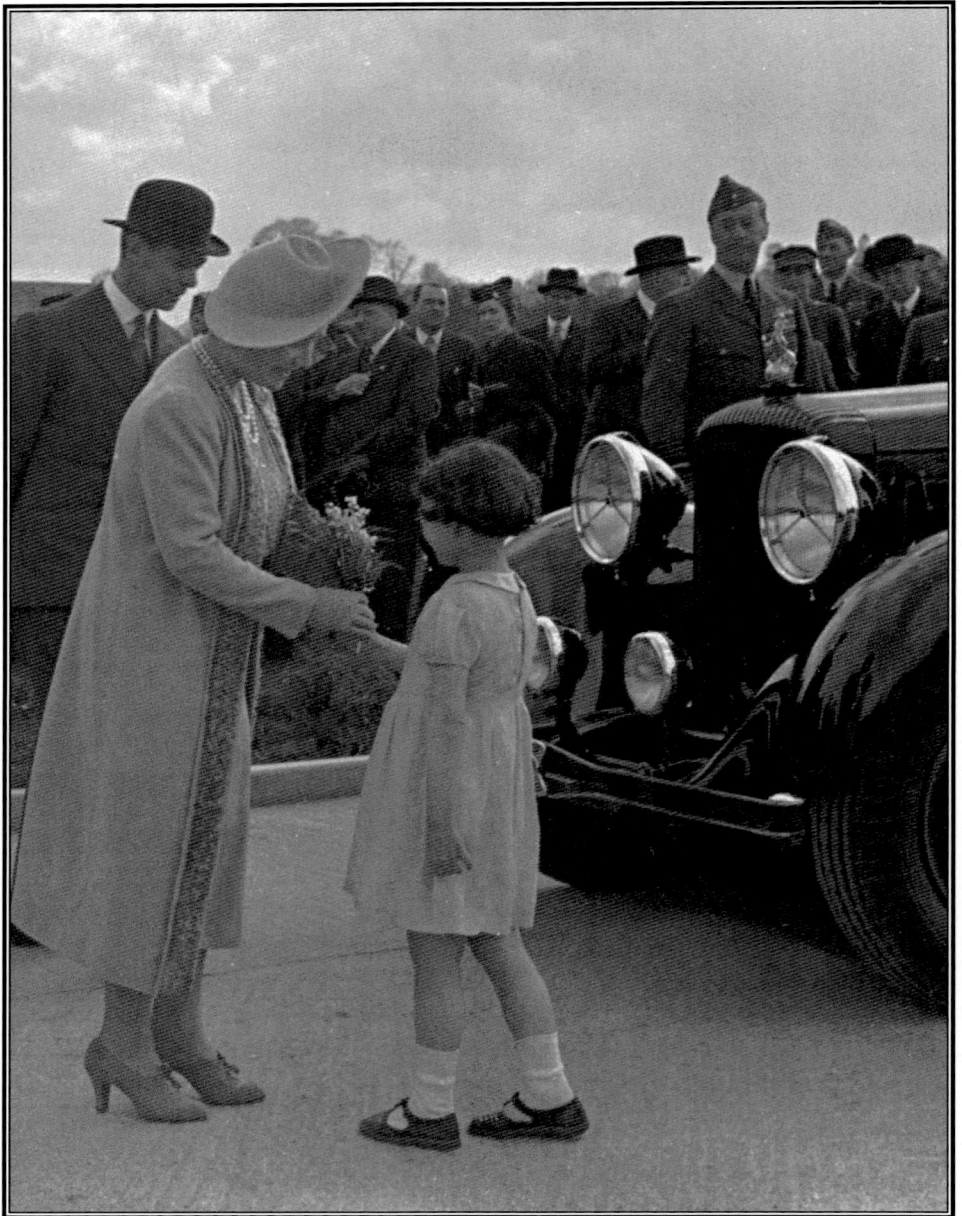

A local girl presents the Queen with a bouquet

Peter and Tony Harcombe at No 2 Stokesby Road in 1937

Tony remembers old Chessington

TONY Harcombe was born on 18th December 1934 and was brought up on the Copt Gilders estate. The family home was at No. 2, Stokesby Road. His mother and father, Marjorie and Hugh, also had another son, Peter, who was 11 years older than Tony.

In 1938, when Tony was aged four, the family moved to the farmhouse at Park Farm, Chalky Lane, opposite the zoo, when Hugh was appointed farm manager. In retirement, Tony recalled his boyhood:

My memories of that early period are few though I do recall Dad holding me by the ankles upside down over the sink in the kitchen and thumping my back to dislodge a swallowed marble.

My mother remembered holding me up to the window, aged two, to see Crystal Palace on fire. We would often walk to the farm, from

Andrew, Marjorie, and Patricia Harcombe at Park Farm, Chessington, in about 1951

Stokesby Road, going by the church and down Green Lane into Chalky Lane at the bottom and on by Monks Cottage into the farmyard. I am not sure who lived at Monks at that time, although Mum and Dad were friends with Rex Pasley and his wife who lived there in the early 1950s.

I remember riding the milk float when the milkman was delivering in Green Lane to the few houses there at the time. It had a pair of

Tony Harcombe in 1937 at Stokesby Road, Chessington

large wheels and a special frame to house a huge churn in the centre. There was a selection of tin-plated measures with long handles to dip milk from the churn and fill containers brought out by the various householders.

Groceries were usually bought at Arthur Pointer's stores in Hook. All dry goods including sugar were scooped from bulk, weighed and wrapped in paper cones made up as they went along. Bread was delivered in their four-wheel horsedrawn van. The van was a bottle green with a nicely written sign on the outside with white on the inside.

Just along from Pointer's, and up a side alley lurked the barber, known to us lads as "Sweeney Todd", to whom I was directed on a fairly regular basis. Sweeney's redeemable feature, to me, anyway, was his ample supply of Beano and Dandy comics to read whilst waiting.

Living on a farm was great for a kid of any age. There were no restrictions and I was able to do things for myself and learn by my mistakes. Soon there was a war on and I went to the little church school, then between the zoo and Barwell Court. The rule then was that if the air-raid siren went before I reached the half-way point, then run home; if more than half-way, run to school.

From primary school I moved to Moor Lane secondary school and this meant a fair walk from Park Farm. When the weather was bad, I caught the 65 bus to Bridge Road to avoid the mud. Moor Lane School was headed by a Mr Loveless and his deputy was Charles Tunicliffe. Ted Wells, father of the actress Julie Andrews, taught woodwork and metalwork. His son, Johnny, was a pupil there at the same time.

I was able to do most work on the farm from an early age and often did tractor driving in the holidays and on summer evenings. I remember my dad saying you can go ploughing on your own but on no account must you attempt to try and restart the engine if you stall it. Come back and find me. I was only 14 and the tractors did not have self-starters in those days. Failure to reset the magneto correctly could result in a broken arm.

During the war, Hans Brick, a tiger tamer at the zoo, kept his pride and joy in an early showman's travelling cage parked in the orchard at Park Farm. It had iron wheels with solid tyres and was divided into two unequal compartments separated by a guillotine gate. Once, Hans and his son, Clive, tried to persuade me to assist them in cleaning out the cage, one compartment at a time, moving the tiger in between. I declined their kind invitation, and told them I didn't like the smell! Many years later, the cage was replaced by a plain wooden

The farmhouse at Park Farm, Chalky Lane, in the time of the Harcombe family's residency in the 1940s

Harvest time at Park Farm and Acre Hill Farm, Chalky Lane, in the late summer of 1952. Farm-hand Charlie Nobbs, left, is seen with farm manager Hugh Harcombe

floor fitted, and the cage used on the farm as a trailer. This work was carried out by builder George "Pop" Oliver and his two sons, Adrian and Roland, who lived out by the Bonesgate pub and who did all the maintenance work on the farm.

Earlier, I'd ride in the back of our milk van up to the big house in the zoo and get a free look around at the animals. The parrots and macaws spaced out on their perches up the driveway would all have something to say as we went by. Sometimes elephants could be seen out on the main road walking in line, each holding on to the tail of the one in front, possibly going to, or coming from, the railway station.

During the war, a few bombs fell on the farm, including a couple of

Harvesting at Park Farm, Chessington, in 1952. Among those on the wagon are Hugh Harcombe and Bill Nobbs (far right). The trailer was previously part of the cage that housed a Chessington Zoo tiger opposite Park Farm, when it was in the prossession of its tamer, Hans Brick

V1 doodlebugs. Nobody was hurt and the damage not serious but the greatest risk were the incendiary bombs, especially during harvest and haymaking. Everyone took turns to look out for the tell-tale smoke.

In a field opposite the front of our house, a searchlight party had been set up by the army after building two Nissen huts for accommodation. They had a big lorry with a generator and this huge arc lamp sitting in its frame in the middle of a rather muddy field.

Traversing the lamp involved walking around in a large circle which rapidly became a very messy business. I have a memory of helping to lay a ring of old bricks to form a path around the perimeter.

To protect the installation there was a fairly ineffective-looking double machine gun with a pan seat and handles to aim it. Mum and Dad were not amused when the lamp happened to be shone into the front windows. I suspect they thought it would fade the wallpaper!

Once, they tried to shoot down a doodebug, but did not succeed.

After the war, when many families were homeless due to the bombing, a wonderful couple moved into the best Nissen hut left by the army. They were very friendly and stayed there some years but I am unable to recall their name.

The land at Park Farm and Acre Hill Farm was owned by Merton College, Oxford, and was farmed by retired naval commander Jack Woodall. However, at the outbreak of war, Commander Woodall was recalled and we saw little of him until the hostilities were over. My father managed the day-to-day running of the farm in conjunction with Mrs Woodall, who was living at Highlands Farm, Leatherhead, and had several other farms to oversee. Park Farm was in the region of 300 acres and stretched, with Acre Hill Farm, from the Epsom road at Malden Rushett to the outskirts of Chessington following the Hogsmill river to a point below St Mary's Church.

Tony Harcombe at Park Farm, at the tractor wheel, with pals and relatives. The lady is Beryl Frost, who lived near Clayton Road, Hook

I went to boarding school until 1950 and did a

Honey, the working horse at Park Farm, waits patiently for instructions from the farmer, Hugh Harcombe in about 1952

Monks Cottage, Chalky Lane, is believed to be Chessington's oldest building, dating back to the 1500s. The zoo's tiger was once kept in a cage near here

year on another farm at Farnham in preparation for a one-year course at Merrist Wood agricultural college, near Guildford, from 1951 to 1952. I started an apprenticeship as an agricultural engineer at Ben Turner & Son, Dorking (latterly Farm Supplies) in 1953. I became a director in the 1960s and retired from there in 1999 and lived in Westcott with my wife, Celia.

FAR LEFT: Hans Brick wrestles with his tigress "Beauty"
LEFT: Five-year-old African lion Habibi at Chessington Zoo in the zoo's formative years

A football team at Fleetwood Boys' School, Garrison Lane, in the 1951-2 season

Buckland Road boyhood memories

DOUGLAS Eves had vivid memories of his time as a boy in Buckland Road where he was involved in much adventure and junior mischief. Writing in the year 2002, he said that his brother was still living in the road.

Douglas Eves and his best pal, Mick Sweeney. Both lived as boys in Buckland Road, Chessington

"The house was one of the 'new age invaders' in the late Forties. In fact it was brand new when we moved from Norbiton in 1949.

"Even with the vast overspill of development going on in the post-war era, Chessington to us was akin to living in the country. To boot, there was a grass verge, back boiler in the lounge, and even a power-point in each room. Our other experience of the 'country' had been in the Cotswolds during the war, as evacuees where my father was billeted for a while.

"The reference to 'country' has always remained a whimsical memory. On the first day of arrival in Chessington, I made my way to the top of 'Gooseberry' Hill which was undeveloped at that time. From there, it was over the top of Chessington North railway station, where I observed Churchfields recreation ground. My actual visualisation of the football players was that of Friesian cows. The fact that some appeared to be moving somewhat faster than others did not deter my escapism dream. It was euphoric to be on high ground in the open fresh air.

"Therefore it was of particular interest to read in *Hook Remembered Again* reference to the "open countryside" and Newlands Way; there being direct affinities with persons as as well as properties. Inevitably, I would suppose, at the age of 63. Living at no 11 Buckland Road was Michael and Tim Sweeney. 'Mick', named after his father, was a great friend. Being of the same age group, we attended Moor Lane Mixed School, and then proceeded to Fleetwood Boys [Garrison Lane].

"In the early days, at about the age of 12, we were contually dreaming up schemes, including a zoo in the back garden of No 11, with an extensive menagerie to rival that of Burnt Stub [Chessington Zoo]. Animals would include a hedgehog, a gerbil, rabbit, the pet cat and a stray dog. This was real 'Just William' stuff.

"Also, with the aid of a John Bull printing outfit, and my tracing the artwork, we published a regular comic of four pages, aptly named 'The Thunder-riders'. It cost one penny (basic) and tuppence for the coloured edition. Tim Sweeney was incorporated into the production team, complete with coloured crayons.

Many happy childhood days were spent, including harvesting the hay in the fields alongside Woodstock Lane. I might add there happened to be another attraction at the age of 14 – a certain Carol Maynard, who lived opposite No 11 in a then newly-built bungalow.

I spent from 1949 to 1957 living in Chessington, there being many down-to-earth, humourous and memorable reminiscences of that era. But with the advent of my National Service, and Mick joining the Merchant Navy, inevitably, our close companionshion became stretched – my going on to marriage, moving to Esher, then to Sussex and the South coast. I regularly return about every six months and always make a point of dropping into the Lucky Rover at Hook for a fine pint in remembrance of Mick, who was tragically killed, and his father who enjoyed a pint or two in both The Cricketers [Clayton Road] and The Lucky. The last time we met was at Michael's funeral. It was on this occasion another memorable experience etched itself into my mind. The day was grey, overcast and drizzly. Standing in the grounds of Kingston Crematorium on my

Fleetwood Boys School football team in 1953. Holding the football is Trevor Watson who went on to sign for Fulham, playing with them from July 1959 to 1964

own in private thoughts, suddenly a gap in the cloud base opened up and presented the unforgettable sound and a glimpse of Concorde. I am not a particularly religious practising person, but that is a spiritual vision locked in my mind forever. The connection? As youngsters, we were avid aircraft spotters, regularly cycling to airfields such as Croydon, Heathrow, Northolt, Fairoaks, Redhill and Gatwick amongst many others. I remember Gatwick, then a grass strip with its beehive control tower. We would sidle along the perimeter track to a small old dilapidated elliptical timber-framed canvas aircraft hangar. In here an old fellow was cannibalising scrap 'piper cubs' leftover by the American forces. Sitting on upturned tea chests and packing cases, each with a mug of tea in hand, he would natter on about his flying experiences. One comment reamins particularly vivid. 'There's your future, lads.' He was pointing to the far end of the grass airfield to Gatwick Racecourse where the grandstand stood alongside the railway line – the site of today's terminal.

"I progressed on to become a member of the 1034 Squadron Surbiton Air Training Corps cadets based off Hook Rise, Tolworth.

A century of service on route 65

An open-top bus on route 65 to Hook in about 1928

*An RT bus on route 71 travels down Victoria Road, Surbiton,
en route to Hook, Chessington, Malden Rushett and
Leatherhead in about 1970*

THE 65 bus was for many decades a familiar sight on the roads of
Chessington, ferrying shoppers to and from Kingston, carrying
children to school and taking visitors to the zoo.

It started its life as the number 105 on 29th March, 1914, when the
service ran from Ealing Broadway via Kew, Richmond and Kingston
to Surbiton Station via Maple Road. In December that year, journeys
continued to run to Surbiton Station but commenced at Argyle Road,
Ealing. In 1920, it was only a Sunday service but became daily in May
1921. On 1st December, 1924, the 105 was renumbered the 65B.

The number 105A began on 24th May, 1914 and its route was Ealing

A 71 to Chessington stops at Hook Library in February 1995

Broadway to Leatherhead. It only ran on Sundays and served South Ealing, Brentford, Kew, Richmond, Kingston, St James' Road, Surbiton Road, Maple Road, Surbiton, Hook, Chessington and Leatherhead. In November 1914, omnibuses on route 105A began at Castlebar, Ealing, and the following month from Argyle Road. Almost a year later, it resumed a service from Ealing Broadway, but thereafter, Argyle Road was the omnibuses' normal departure point.

In July 1919, the service ran from Ealing to only Hook, Mondays to Saturdays, but the route was extended on Sundays to Leatherhead, presumably to transport London visitors to the Surrey countryside. The service was withdrawn for four months in January 1920 but by April that year, it was back running between Ealing and Leatherhead on Sundays. It was registered more simply as route 65 on 1st December 1, 1924.

In the first decade of the service, omnibuses used to terminate at

Kew   Richmond
Ham   Kingston
Surbiton   Hook Road
Chex Gilders Estate

65

CHESSINGTON ZOO

OLD 768

An RT model 65 bus to the zoo in about 1970

the North Star, Hook. To enable return journeys to be made to Ealing, the 'buses used to be reversed from Hook Road into Orchard Road so they were pointed in the right direction. The terminus was changed to the White Hart pub, Hook, on 28th January, 1931. The buses to Hook only were usually numbered 65A; those running to Leatherhead were the 65s. Before the construction of Leatherhead bus garage, the town's terminus was The Bull pub.

On 27th May, 1936, the route was altered between Kingston and Surbiton. Instead of Penrhyn Road, the 65s in future were to use Fairfield Road and Villiers Road.

In 1943, the 65s on Sunday mornings only ran to Hook but continued to Leatherhead in the afternoons.

An old London horsebus, which used to operate in Brixton, was given a new lease of life transporting passengers to and from Chessington South Station and Chessington Zoo. This picture was taken on 27th March 1944

By 1968, Chessington Zoo was a regular terminus for many journeys not continuing on to Malden Rushett and Leatherhead.

Some school journeys were extended to the Fox and Hounds (now the Shy Horse).

In February 1987, route 65 only ran on Sundays to Chessington Zoo but continued as a night service from Ealing to the zoo as N65.

In the late 1990s, Armchair travel took over the daytime service but its route had already been shortered to the stretch between Ealing and Kingston.

The 65A begain its life on 11th October, 1950, running from Ealing (Argyle Road) to Hook and then Bridge Road and Church Lane to the new Copt Gilders estate where it terminated at the green.

On New Year's Eve, 1966, the service was extended from Copt Gilders to the zoo. But if heavy traffic had led to delays, some journeys still turned around at Copt Gilders. A Sunday service in late 1966 also served Copt Gilders and the buses went on to the zoo and

A fleet of Routemaster buses on routes 71 and 65 seen at Kingston bus station, then sited next to Kingston Station, in April 1980. The picture was taken by bus enthusiast and author, Roy Hobbs

Leatherhead. The 65A was formally withdrawn on 29th November 1968.

The 71 began its life on 3rd October, 1934, with a Sunday service between Kings Cross and Southall, covering Notting Hill Gate, Shepherds Bush, Acton and Ealing. This was withdrawn in 1939 but the number was used from 11th January, 1950 for a service between Richmond and Kingston. From 1951, the service was extended to Hammersmith.

The 71 was used on a service between Sunbury and Hammersmith (via Kingston) from May 1959, and in 1960, the route was extended to East Acton.

In 1964, the 71 route was Kington to East Acton, and in 1966 from Kingston to Hammersmith.

On 11th November, 1967, the service was altered to Richmond to Kingston and a year later, on 30th November, 1968, the Chessington service was commenced. Those debut journeys were from Leatherhead to Kingston on Sundays and to Richmond on other days. Most journeys therefater ran between Chessington Zoo and Richmond, with a service to the Fox and Hounds, Malden Rushett, at peak times. In the 1990s, London United ran the service.

A 265 bus operated between 1952 and 1980, with several alterations to its route during that time. It started on 14th May, 1952, running from East Acton to Hook and the Copt Gilders estate, Chessington, (Mondays to Saturdays).

In 1965, it is listed as having a Richmond-Kingston-Chessington route. This service was withdrawn on 26th September, 1980. Thereafter, the 265 conveyed passengers around Putney, and Roehampton, its service extended to Tolworth Broadway in 1991.

The 714 Green Line used to run through Chessington and Hook. This service began just after the Second World War, starting with a route from Dorking to Baker Street, London. It was extended to Luton in September 1951. Heavy congestion led to the service running only between Dorking and Victoria from October 1977 and Horsham to Victoria from August 1980.

In 1987, there were occasional extensions beyond Horsham to

Brighton, after the service was taken over by London and Country South West in September 1986.

On 20th June, 1987, some people north of Kingston said a final farewell to the 714, after it was withdrawn between Kingston and Victoria. The 714 (and the 514 which ran in conjunction) were withdrawn on 29th June, 1991.

The 465 (note the inclusion of the '65' in the numbering) took over the 714 service, serving all points between Kingston and Dorking.

In more recent years, the 65 bus has been operating a night service only between Ealing and Chessington Zoo, helping to perpetuate the long history of the route spanning more than 100 years.

London tram no.1858 for many years was on show at Chessington Zoo. The much-loved vehicle was moved to the Tramway Museum Society at Carlton Colville, Leics, in April 1964. Note the rather apt destination board which reads 'Elephant and Castle'

About the author

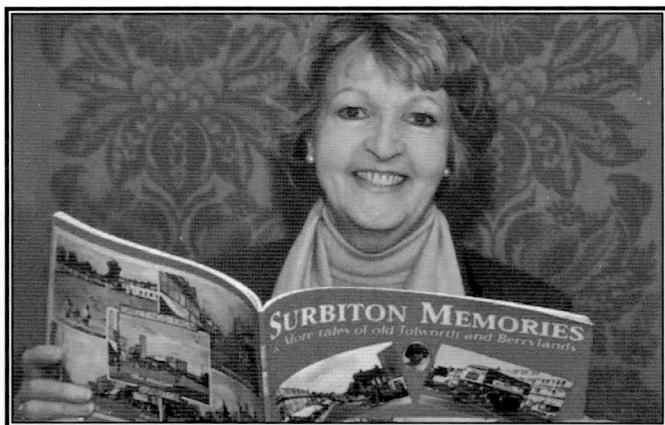

Actress Penelope Keith, of The Good Life fame, reading the author's Surbiton Memories book. The television series was based on the town

MARK Davison spent his working life in local journalism, starting his career at the Kingston Borough News, where he was greatly influenced by its regular columnist Margaret Bellars who compiled features on the district's past. In more recent years. he linked up with June Sampson to produce *Kingston in the Fifties*, a local best-seller. Mark's research highlights include tracing original pupils of Enid Blyton when she lived and taught in Hook Road, and finding, for the first time, the house where novelist Thomas Hardy lived in Hook Road when Far From the Madding Crowd was completed in 1874.

Other books in the series include:
Hook Remembered
Chessington Remembered
Long Ditton Remembered
Surbiton Bombed
Hook Remembered Again
Tolworth Remembered,
Fireside Tales of Tolworth
Kingston in the Fifties
Surbiton Bombed
The Olympic Flame Comes to Hook
Please call or email to check availability

Email mark.davison1@virgin.net to find out how to purchase a copy of his books. Or call 01737 221215